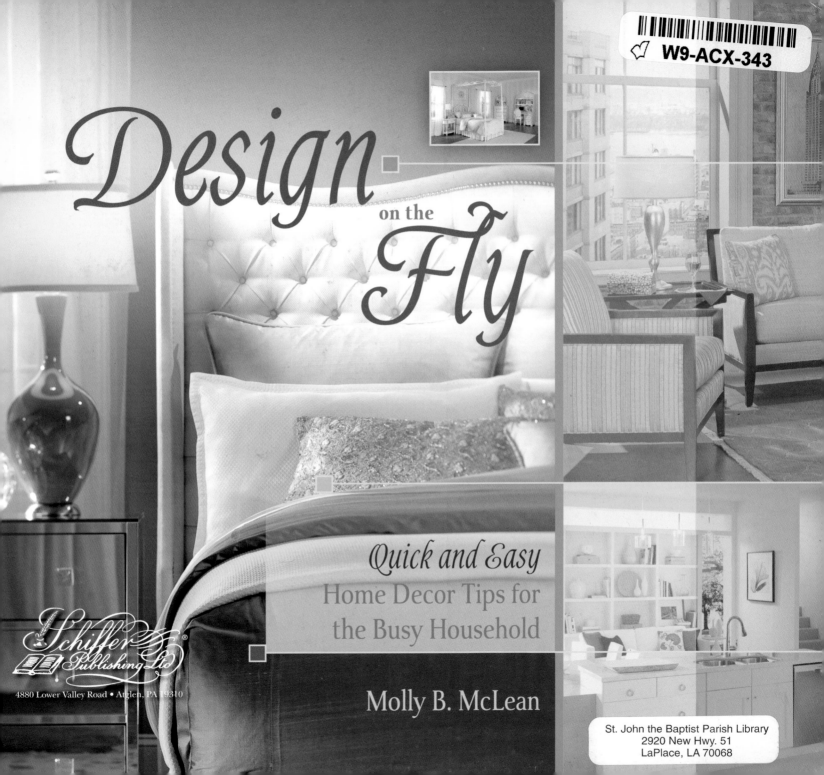

Design
on the
Fly

Quick and Easy
Home Decor Tips for
the Busy Household

Schiffer
Publishing Ltd

4880 Lower Valley Road • Atglen, PA 19310

Molly B. McLean

To my little wildfire Ella.
Dream Big and run with it.

Copyright © 2013 by Molly B. McLean

Library of Congress Control Number: 2013938831

Designed by Danielle D. Farmer
Type set in Alys/Adobe Fangsong Std/Conduit ITC

ISBN: 978-0-7643-4433-6
Printed in China

Published by Schiffer Publishing, Ltd.
4880 Lower Valley Road
Atglen, PA 19310
Phone: (610) 593-1777; Fax: (610) 593-2002
E-mail: Info@schifferbooks.com

For our complete selection of fine books on this and related subjects, please visit our website at www.schifferbooks.com. You may also write for a free catalog.

This book may be purchased from the publisher. Please try your bookstore first.

We are always looking for people to write books on new and related subjects. If you have an idea for a book, please contact us at proposals@schifferbooks.com.

Schiffer Publishing's titles are available at special discounts for bulk purchases for sales promotions or premiums. Special editions, including personalized covers, corporate imprints, and excerpts can be created in large quantities for special needs. For more information, contact the publisher.

In Europe, Schiffer books are distributed by
Bushwood Books
6 Marksbury Ave.
Kew Gardens
Surrey TW9 4JF England
Phone: 44 (0) 20 8392 8585; Fax: 44 (0) 20 8392 9876
E-mail: info@bushwoodbooks.co.uk
Website: www.bushwoodbooks.co.uk

Acknowledgments

A VERY BIG THANK YOU
to the homeowners who opened their doors and let me
peruse their space with a camera!

Landon and Shelly Bordeaux
George and Fran Zenisky
Ben and Holly Hughes
Buddy and Cassandra Britt
Jeff and Ashley Ward
Laurie Leonhardt
Charles and Lorraine Sherrill
Rose Price
Hampton and Jo Burgess

To my childhood best friend, who offered her assistance and kept
reworking her space and taking photos until we got it just right. Melissa
Garcia, thank you so much for being so wonderful!

To all the associates at Albion who take fabulous photos, make lots
of spreadsheets, and don't mind my endless emails: Miles Barefoot,
Wendy High, Teresa Slane, Britt Johnson.

To the people who live with me and are related whether they want to be
or not! My husband David, for doing all the things on the computer that
I can't figure out and the endless reworking, resaving, and redistributing
of endless photographs. Ella, for being an inspiration and continuously
providing me with more hoops to learn how to jump through and more
tasks to learn how to juggle. She is why mommy gets it all done! My
parents, Wanda and Bryant Herring, for last minute babysitting and
coming to the rescue in the eleventh hour. Amy Herring, my sister-
in-law, for fabulous creativity in coming up with a title for this book!

And thank you to all the girls I've been on the journey of mommy-hood
with! To all who asked how the book was going and offered to assist
with Miss Ella. This book has been quite a journey and I hope to take it
again! And to the ladies at preschool: I don't know how anyone could
be as fabulous as you are; thank you for making Ella's days so wonderful
while I stared at a computer screen and thought of fabulous things to
write down!

Contents

Before having my daughter, I had no idea what designing in an efficient manner was. As an interior designer, my life has always revolved around color, ideas, and inspiration. It was quite different before she came into my life. I could simply take all the time I needed to research a space, make plans for the idea, and leave projects unattended until I returned to them.

I have always known that a beautiful space is important for creating a beautiful life. Our environment has such a huge impact on our lives, and we don't even realize it. The color of a room and the way a space is designed can have an effect on you in different ways. So, of course, I shrugged off my friends' notions, who would tell me that when I had children, my house would not look the same.

Of course, like my own child, my strong will was out to prove them wrong. I would have a well designed, organized space, and prove that it was possible. Well, maybe not organized, but you get the point.

It is, in fact, possible, but there are a few places where you do have to bend. It may not look like a magazine cover at all times, but, with the right pieces and the right mindset, it's easy to tuck those toys away in no time, so, even if a stuffed animal is peeking from under the coffee table, it still looks like grown-ups live there. Of course, when it's just you and the kids, by all means let them roll with it, but make sure they clean up their mess afterwards!

This book will have some great ideas for time management, with quick and easy tips that make a big impact on a space, and it will be humorous. After all, being a mother is humorous; being a busy woman just seems to go along with the territory. I honestly don't know if I've ever met a woman that wasn't busy.

I will say, I am not a hyper-organizer, so this book is probably not going to have a lot of examples worthy of an organizational expert. If you know where to find a pair of socks, however, you are ahead in the game.

It is hard to find the time for decorating the home when you are always busy. Life can get in the way, and sometimes there are little monsters tugging at your pants leg. So, whether there is one on the way or several in the way, decorating in an efficient manner can help you create a warm and pleasing space for the entire family.

This journey will be an exciting one, because life is exciting and we are ready to get started. Love the life you live....it starts at home. So let's go!

1

Welcome:
Entrances

A single overhead light and oil-rubbed hardware exudes the rustic feel of this 1920s bungalow's round top door.

A simple door knocker accents the front door well.

*Y*ou're finally home! You know that feeling of relief as you pull into your driveway after being gone all day, whether it was to work or just a day out with the kids? Someone is either throwing a tantrum or you just can't wait to get out of the car.

To welcome you home, a beautiful entrance is a must. Once you step onto the stoop or front porch, relief washes over you and it's like you hear the heavens open up and the sound of hallelujahs. You've been there. We all have!

A lime green door brightens an entrance.

Bright yellow is a fun color for a door on a brick ranch home. White frames the door and creates a visual break between the red brick and yellow door.

A portico over a red door is a welcoming entrance to this home. The red adds a pop of color to the exterior color scheme.

So let's talk about what makes up the entrance and how to get a beautiful one in the shortest amount of time possible. The front door is the centerpiece of your home's exterior and it makes the first impression. The color on the door as well as the plantings and arrangement define the entrance as its own space, giving a prelude to what is inside.

So often we forget about this element, but a simple adjustment can change the entire look of your house. The entrance usually tells the story of what lies inside. If the outside is a mess, chances are the inside is too.

A pop of color will make your door stand out and create an inviting welcome for what lies beyond. Some of the most beautiful doors I have seen are a deep barn red against a white frame house. Red doesn't have to be limited to white homes, though. Brick houses can also benefit from a door in the right shade of red. Black is always a good standby, but bold doors, such as those in eggplant, lime green, and blues, are as equally pleasing visually, if in the right setting. A white clapboard cottage is a good example of where a lime green or sea blue door can be used to make a stunning impact.

Painting the door is quick and easy. It's like instant gratification for the exterior! You get a lot of bang for your buck with this one simple change. You only need a quart of paint and it takes a couple coats to create good color after a primer.

If your child is in the toddler phase, then this will need to be done during nap time or an episode of "Dora;" you can always use the dog as a distraction, as long as they are within plain sight! But sometimes a project can't be done quickly, or your kids are too much of a distraction once the paint brushes and buckets are out. If you are one of the fortunate ones who have family, relatives, or even a drop-in play care, then by all means take advantage of them when you are tackling a big project.

But for those of us, myself included, who just assume we can do anything with anyone hanging on our leg, when there's a will there's a way... so let's get to it. This project can be completed in a couple of hours or less.

Now that the door is painted, we can move onto the next phase of the entrance which is the surroundings.

Two ferns placed in matching urns provide a quick and simple way to add class to an entrance.

TIP

Need it Now

Purchase ready-made pots of several plantings at your local hardware store or garden center instead of assembling your plantings. After all, if your child is scaling the ladder while in the garden center, you will probably be asked to leave and time will be of the essence!

Flower pots extending the steps as well as ferns by the front door are quite beautiful in this southern home. Buy hanging baskets and place them in pots to cut down on time. Just remember to remove the hangers and keep them watered during dry months.

Who doesn't love a porch swing? If space allows, kids and grown-ups alike can enjoy swinging in the cool breeze. A few pillows add color to the porch.

For a more formal look, add two faux topiaries in urns to create a symmetrical feel.

If you have shrubs that are starting to protrude over the porch, cut those bushes down. Overgrown bushes can have such a negative impact on the front of the home. If they have gotten too big, then you can always prune them or remove them and replace them with smaller plantings. If you choose to prune, you may want to do a bit of research on your type of plants before you start.

Now to my favorite part, which is adding the color. This can be done by using flowers in pots on each side of the entrance in varying heights. For an asymmetrical look, a large pot of foliage and one or two smaller pots in front creates an appealing look.

A pair of topiaries creates a more formal look, and something as simple as a pair of boxwoods or dwarf Alberta spruce trees will make an impact while achieving the formal idea.

Pots are like doors, they come in all colors. If you've got the right combination it can make the front of your entire house pop.

Being from the south, front porches are predominant where I live, but, would you believe, I don't have one! If you are fortunate enough to have a large porch, then by all means use every square inch to draw the eye to the front of your home with, for example, sprawling ferns and groups of rocking chairs. But just remember, the more that is on the porch, the more that will need watering during hot months. So take into consideration the amount of time you want to spend with plant upkeep. If you're like me and digging in the dirt is therapeutic, then this is a good way to reduce some stress. Insert ear buds and begin.

Rocking chairs, greenery, and even the address on your door can either welcome a guest or send the signal that you want them to go away. And you may want to send them packing, if it's relatives you really don't care to see!

Opposite In a simple setting such as this, a topiary of ivy and a statue create an asymmetrical look for the entrance. On this brick, two story home, the focal point is the beautiful greenery above the door. Bold numbers and a brass kick plate make this door stand out.

For the stoop-style entrance, keep it simple and use the "less is more" approach. If there is too much going on outside, then the inside probably looks the same.

Something as simple as two flower pots can add personality to your front door. A fresh coat of paint can breathe a whole new life into the entire scheme of your home.

New hardware, lighting, and a kick plate give life to a front door no matter what the age of your home.

Add a pretty door knocker, mailbox, and nice, scripted numbers for your address.

Lighting is also an important element of the entrance. If you've got a rusty old lantern barely dangling by its chord, then it is time to say adios! If your fixture is in pretty good shape but needs a facelift then whip out the spray paint. Just one piece that looks unkempt can throw off the whole look and, conversely, just one simple change can make a huge impact on your design.

A brightly colored wreath contrasts well with this black front door. You can quickly make one yourself or buy one at most any craft store to save time. For additional pizzazz wrap a garland of flowers through a store-bought wreath.

Time Crunch Entrances

■ GOT AN HOUR?

- Add pre-made plantings to the door in groups of three for a casual look or two topiaries on each side for a more formal look.
- Add a couple of boxwoods to two new pots; trim them round to give the appearance of a small topiary.
- Add new address numbers to your front door or above the door if space allows.
- Replace the door mat.

■ GOT TWO HOURS?

- Give the front door a fresh coat of paint, maybe in a new color.
- Change out a worn and dated light fixture, or remove and spray paint existing one.
- Trim the shrubs nearest to the front door. An electric hedge clipper is the quickest. If you're not sure of the shape, research it online before you begin.

■ GOT A WEEKEND?

- Stain the concrete on your front porch.
- Repaint the porch or stoop, if paint is chipping away.
- Replace overgrown or sparse shrubs.

Wall decals, put up in a flash, make an impact in this foyer.

2

Where are the keys?
Foyers

This bench is a place to have a seat and stow away the shoes. It works well at the back or front entrance and minimizes clutter. A colorful cushion adds some personality.

TIP

The Toys Have Taken Over

Always have baskets in places where toys seem to linger. This way they're put away quickly and blend with the decor. No one can function in a completely chaotic environment!

The foyer or entry way, as it is often called, will be the first view of the inside of your home. Even though a lot of time is not spent in this area and it is more of a pass-through, make it warm and inviting. This may also need to be a place to corral the family's shoes, car keys, and coats, and a few toys are bound to make their way into this area. You may not spend a lot of time in this space, but you need to make this room work. It needs to be both visually pleasing and functional, because this space is the connecting piece to adjoining rooms.

A pair of lamps and a mirror over a dresser lightens the space and provides a place for storage and to drop off keys and other miscellaneous items.

Almost any type of cabinet or furniture piece with a flat surface can work in the foyer.

Many homes do not have a separate foyer, so in that case you have to create one, which is quite easy to do with a little imagination. Here in the south, the ranch home is very popular and in recent years builders seem to forgo the foyer. I have also lived in one of these cookie cutter homes. I often referred to our neighborhood as the mill village, so I am well aware of what you have to work with!

There are a few basics that every foyer needs: a mirror, lighting, a table or bench, and a door mat. A mirror will not only reflect light into a dark space, but also lets you take one last, quick check on your way out the door. A piece of furniture, whether it is a console, chest, or bookcase, anchors the space and provides a place to drop keys and mail.

A floating sofa can create a visual wall if your home opens up to the family room and there is no separate space for an entry way. If space allows, add a couple of chairs and a small table on the main wall behind the sofa to catch keys and miscellaneous items from those coming in the front door, and a mat for wiping their feet.

A console with an open base provides space to add baskets to house each family member's shoes. If you are tight on space and funds allow, have a custom piece built that has hooks for coats and shelving for shoes. This keeps the space uncluttered and everyone's belongings within easy reach.

Again, if you do not have a wall and are creating a visual foyer, an open book case can do the trick. If you go with this approach, however, it needs to be a built-in unit, anchored to the floor to prevent accidents caused by climbing tots.

Always look up as well; walls are prime real estate for placing items up and away. Drawing the eye upward gives the illusion of a larger space.

Don't forget about personal touches like family photographs and artwork. The foyer is a wonderful place to showcase photographs in an arrangement on the wall, much like an art gallery.

If space allows in your foyer, provide a seat!

Photos in black and white make an impact.

Photos look less cluttered when in similar colored frames and arranged close together. You can continuously add to the collection over time and, whether they are black-and-white or colored photos, they appear more visually appealing in similarly colored frames, such as all black, white, or silver. This is the perfect way to showcase candid photographs and your family in the stairwell.

Before filling the walls up with nail holes arrange frames on the floor first and then place them on the wall. If you won't get too excited about them being rearranged, by all means let the little ones assist with laying them out on the floor. It is much like a puzzle and they will enjoy helping you as well as seeing the different photos. Children love to be in the middle of everything and, though it may take a little bit longer to do, it provides some quality mommy time.

Lighting is an extremely important element in the foyer and entryway. If you have some hideous brass fixture that is missing a few pieces or just looks like it materialized out of 1983, then it is time for a change. If the fixture has good character, you can remove it, spray paint it white or black, and re-hang it. If it is not a pleasing design or in good shape, it may be time to say goodbye. (I actually spray painted a chandelier while it was still hanging up, but I don't recommend this particular way because I don't want to be responsible for anyone spray painting their furniture!)

Always research before you head out to purchase items for your home. Not only will this create less frustration, but time in the store is time you could be working on a project at home. So, instead of spending time on Facebook® or Twitter® (I know this is hard!), take a look online or in a magazine to see what you like. Make sure what you select fits with the rest of your home. An ultra-modern pendant may not swing well with your Craftsman bungalow.

Don't forget the flooring. I know all too well that some homes do not have a separate foyer and that the front door sometimes opens into a living room. I refer to this style as the builder box. Our first home was a builder box, so I am acquainted with this style and with the need to insert some personality. If this is the situation in your home, use an area rug to prevent too much wear on your carpet. It can be secured with carpet tape until you can install a hard surface such as hardwood or tile.

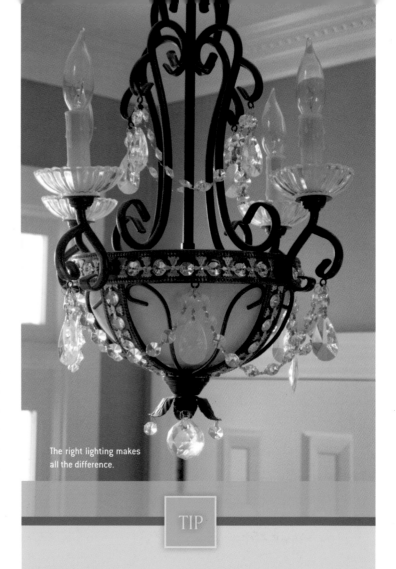

The right lighting makes all the difference.

TIP

To prevent Google® overload, make sure you key in something specific, such as "photos of foyers with wood floors and blue walls," versus keying in "foyers." This way you will narrow down the search to what particularly interests you instead of getting sidetracked while gazing over thousands of photos. No one has the time for this either, unless you plan on staying up all night!

Don't forget the floor! A brightly colored rug adds a pop of color to this foyer and ties the adjoining rooms together.

Homes with separate foyers can be impacted by using a patterned rug that entertains the eye. Choose one that is appealing for your space, whether it be bold or neutral. A runner works well for narrow corridors. Make sure to choose a flat nap on the rug for this area so the door can swing over it easily.

If there is no coat closet, a skinny coat rack can fit in tight spaces. Also, a built-in can multi-task as the coat rack, shoe rack, and toy shelter. With kids, there are toys, so teach them at a young age how to put their things away.

Wall color is not only one of the largest elements in any space, it also provides the most impact, giving you the biggest bang for your buck.

TIP

Purchase a paint fan. It will be one of your best investments if you have several rooms to paint. They can be found at hardware stores and paint suppliers and are inexpensive.

Bold colors in the foyer pack a big design punch. When you are selecting a color for your foyer, remember, however, that it needs to transition well to the adjoining rooms. You probably don't want a dill pickle green foyer opening up to a flame red dining room, unless your name is St. Nick. All rooms need to transition from one to another. This does not mean you have to keep the same theme throughout your home, but you do need to have one common element, whether it is the trim or a color that you use in each space to tie rooms together, with an item such as a piece of artwork, a pillow, or another accessory.

When selecting the wall color, pull colors from artwork or furnishings. Don't just pull a color out of the air, saying, "I think I will paint the family room orange." Chances are it is not going to work. Color needs to have some thought put into it. If you just cannot visualize, there are online tools available so you can paint a wall virtually. Though they will be a slightly different variation, they will give you a good idea of how your room will look. When I am unsure of a color, one trick I use is to drape a piece of fabric of the same tones in the room, whether it is fabric sample or a blanket, so I can get a better idea.

Don't be afraid of color. An entire house of beige is boring! Please don't be boring. Life is too short to live in a boring house!

More tips on how to paint quickly are found in the next chapter.

A white piece brightens this spot, creates another place to display favorite things, and works overtime as a storage piece. And yes, kids live here!

Time Crunch Foyers

■ GOT AN HOUR?

- Select a new wall color.
- Hang a mirror over a console table.
- Browse the Internet for a rug that makes a statement and purchase it.
- Place a basket near the door for keys and mail.
- Change out the foyer light for a new one. Make sure you read all the directions and turn off the breaker!
- Add artwork beside a mirror in an arrangement.

■ GOT TWO HOURS?

- Tape off the foyer for painting.
- Prep and caulk any existing holes in walls.
- Arrange a side chair and table.
- Add names to storage baskets with cute tags found at craft stores and/or add the initial of each family member, hanging it from a ribbon to mark their belongings.

■ GOT A WEEKEND?

- Paint the foyer.
- Paint the trim a fresh coat of white or cream.
- Lay a new floor.

Life is a circus!

3

Take a Break!
**Living
and
Family
Rooms**

Add color to a neutral scheme by using greenery and plantings, real or faux.

he living and family rooms are known as the gathering places of the home. This space is a center of activity, from reading a magazine to using the computer, playing games, coloring, or vegging out in front of the TV. Kids never wind down, but the adults attempt to in this space. As the catchall activity space, this room needs to be functional, comfortable, and, of course, pretty! So let's talk about this space. How do you make it look visually pleasing while also being kid- and pet-friendly, and how do you do this as quickly as possible, so you don't have design projects going on for months?

Clockwise In a modern setting, bare windows create a more open feel for this space. | On a hard surface such as concrete or wood, a rug is important for anchoring furniture and creating a place for conversation. | Adding pieces to the tops of furniture adds visual height in a space with tall ceilings.

Start with the major pieces in this room such as the sofa, chairs, and bookshelves. You will want to work your pieces around the room's focal points which are most likely the TV and fireplace. Comfort is important in this space. Furniture arrangement will affect the comfort of conversation as well as viewing the TV. A sofa across from two chairs, or two loveseats across from each other, creates a comfortable seating arrangement.

A comfy sofa makes for a softer landing and lots of pillows not only provide extra cushion, but can add pops of color as well. A good rule of thumb when considering the amount of space you have to work with is to figure out what your largest piece of furniture is or where the focal point is going to be. For example, the fireplace or the television may be the focal

point; whatever it is, you work around it. The main pieces of furniture would include the sofa and chairs.

Here's a formula that works: the main piece or grouping of furniture can take up about 40 percent of the room, leaving about 10 to 15 percent for other pieces and 40 percent for walking space.

If you have a tall ceiling to work with, you will need some larger pieces to draw the eye upward, so your furniture will not seem overwhelmed. This can also be achieved with artwork groupings above a particular piece, giving visual height.

Window treatments, throw pillows and accessories all complete a space and make it feel less sparse and more pulled together.

Mix patterns for added personality.

Accent chairs tie a room's scheme together.

TIP

Need it Now

Move that sofa all around the room by using a sheet or towel placed under its feet. In this way, you can get it done without breaking your back and your children or cat can ride on the sofa, so you won't trip over them! Make it a game. This little trick works well over carpet where furniture movers are more difficult to use. It also prevents the scratching of hardwood floors.

When using multiple patterns, ensure that they go together by using a print with a floral pattern or a fabric of three colors next to one of two.

There's more to seating than just the sofa. Chairs are also an important element in this space. I admit, I have a thing for chairs. Chairs and shoes. I'm not sure where that combination came from, but I guess we all have our quirks.

While creating an appealing environment, there needs to be enough seating for each of your guests. The accent chair is that one pop of color that can bring the entire room together and incorporate your personality. Bold patterns can enable you to add flair to the space.

A very sleek, modern chair of metal or natural woods works for a minimalist style. The more traditional style can derive its looks from an accent piece in damask, paisley, or another bold pattern. If you have too much pattern going on, then different textures will be the way to go. Create a feast for the eyes, but don't overindulge with an all-you-can-eat buffet! The statement "less is more" is true. I believe in color and accessories, but don't overdo it.

TIP

Inexpensive Update

Purchase a chair from the consignment or thrift shop and recover in a vibrant pattern. If you are fortunate enough to have an heirloom chair, this will be more meaningful. Incorporate a bit of history into your design, and spice it up a bit. Look for good structure and consider the overall design of the chair. Overlook the hideous fabric. Smaller chairs only need about 3-4 yards of fabric to reupholster, so they are the inexpensive and work well in about any space for the extra punch of color.

Tables near major pieces are a must if you will be eating in the family room.

Also keep in mind that the family room is casual; therefore, make sure there is a small table or two nearby for placing cups or plates. Most of us dine in the family room at some point during the day, so, to prevent spills, make sure you have adequate pieces, such as end tables or coffee tables, for cups and place them within arm's reach of the seating. My family often snacks in the family room, and there are spills and there are messes. But this is a family space and is not meant to be covered in plastic. So, I keep a bottle of spot cleaner handy to quickly remove spilled drink or food. Also, if you have kids, chances are there will be crumbs in the sofa. Just make sure you vacuum this out during your routine cleaning to keep from having an infestation of grossness!

Color can do wonders for any space. Breathe new life into your current furnishings with fresh pillows in various patterns and textures. Have an idea of the colors you are looking for before ever stepping into the store. Take a swatch of something similar to the color of your sofa whether it is a paint chip or an existing pillow, so you have the color scheme in mind. Also, shop where you know they have various styles of pillows instead of going from store to store; this will help save some valuable time. If you have to spend an entire day trying to find five pillows, it is not only daunting but takes the fun out of the project.

Shopping just isn't quite the same once kids come along, unless someone is willing to watch them for you. So now it's more of a mission than a therapeutic session and, at times, it can be quite frustrating. That is why it's best to be ready for the mission before you start. This creates a lot less headaches. You don't want to get annoyed and leave empty handed.

TIP

Some Key Points with Pillows

- *Group in odd numbers.*
- *Tie various colors in a room together with several pillows.*
- *A beige sofa in a soft blue room will pop with a couple of blue, patterned pillows, a couple of tan pillows, and one extra pillow for an additional punch of color. This could be chocolate brown or a deeper blue depending on your scheme.*
- *Different sizes and shapes make for an interesting look. You need not stay with all the same size and color.*
- *Purchase two pillows in one color, two more in an additional color, and one accent pillow if you're not sure.*

Left to right A white media center which coordinates with the trim has the look of a custom built-in. | A media center can perform double duty as a place for displays as well as housing for the TV and equipment.

Television has definitely improved over the years and, while it still reminds me of a black hole in the wall, we all have them and love them. The television isn't exactly the most beautiful piece in any setting; however, with the latest technology they have improved in looks by far. Some of the low television tables are aesthetically pleasing, but, if you have toddlers, they are not high enough to keep sticky hands out of reach, so you will most likely have sticky finger smudges all over the screen.

In this case, either mount the TV high or use a taller piece of furniture. Remember to anchor the TV so your toddler will not pull it down on him or herself. Straps for the TV can be found at most hardware stores and where electronics are sold.

A built-in, made for the TV, is a great way to showcase it, store the extra entertainment pieces, and even have room for displays above. They are often wall units and do double duty as multi-purpose pieces. Adjustable bookshelves can work the same way.

Any piece of furniture over two feet tall needs to be strapped to the wall with furniture straps to prevent tipping on toddlers. See the resource guide for where to purchase these.

A refurbished dresser provides a stand for the TV and extra storage.

An end table with drawers and shelving provides an extra place to stow away magazines and toys. Think multi-purpose when you are purchasing new items.

Make a small space appear more expansive by adding a large mirror. Place it behind a piece of furniture to keep it from toppling over or driving you nuts with fingerprints!

Accessorize! Much like a great outfit, a room also needs accessories to pull the space together. This is my favorite part of design. I've been collecting since I was a child, so, hopefully, I won't become a borderline hoarder. This is where you can showcase your favorite things. Yes, at one time you were able to leisurely stroll through the estate sale and antique fair, but that's not really the case anymore if you have kids.

I know what you are thinking. This lady is crazy. There is some truth to that! The thought may be that, if you have kids, you should limit everything. This is just not true! Make your accessories do double duty. Most homeowners devote a lot of time to choosing something beautiful for their space. While this is a great idea, if you're as busy as most of us are, you don't have time to go to four stores looking for the perfect green lampshade. But at one time, maybe you were able to lovingly select a collection of McCoy pottery piece by piece or some other treasure. Well, you can still display them. More tips about this subject can be found in the Up, Up and Away Chapter. However, if you're adding to your accessories, paring down, or starting over, think about pieces that have a dual purpose, because, if you have kids, it needs to be functional *and* aesthetically pleasing for the space.

Baskets and containers will be your dearest decorating friends. Buy baskets that can house remotes, DVDs, or CDs (possibly together), and baskets to keep the toys corralled. Most living and family rooms are havens for clutter. Shallow baskets that slide under the sofa work well for storing magazines and coloring books. Buy a coffee table that can house baskets underneath or an ottoman that flips up and has a place for storage. The basic coffee table, with an open space underneath, can work as well with pretty storage containers. Measure your space before you buy your containers and take a tape measure with you so you're not guessing if it will fit.

Baskets beneath the coffee table stow away toys and coordinate with the room's scheme.

TIP

When purchasing containers to house clutter, make sure to measure the space in which you want them to fit and write your measurements down. Take a tape measure with you to the store to ensure you have an accurate fit and you're not guessing. You don't have time for guessing, so take the measurements!

Panels go up quickly and elongate the windows without being too heavy.

WINDOWS

Now let's talk about windows. Some spaces need window treatments because they are just too bare otherwise. Uncovered windows, though, can work in an industrial or modern type space.

More traditional spaces appear to look naked if the windows are bare, so a simple treatment, such as a Roman shade or panel, works well without making it look overdone. Don't hate me for this statement, but it is probably time to say goodbye to the swags and cascades in your home and opt for a more updated, simple look such as panels on each side. You will need to determine the necessary treatments based on the size of your window and the style of your room.

In your mind you're thinking, my child will just pull them down, swing from them, or climb them. If that's a problem, maybe we could look into a rope design or add a ladder beside the window! The easiest way to handle this problem is by hanging the cords high enough where they are out of reach and, if using panels, let the children know they are mommy and daddy's, and that you do not mess with their toys so they should leave yours alone. Or possibly call Super Nanny to rectify the issue!

Again, to cut down on store time, browse the Internet by keying in your favorite store and find out what type of window treatments they offer. You can get design ideas before you set out on the quest for the perfect window treatment. Searching on the Internet can be time consuming as well, so instead of typing in something as broad as "window treatment," Google® something like "family room, navy and white color scheme," etc., depending on what you're working with. You will get an array of photos for ideas.

Layered window treatments add texture to this space and a small desk in the corner provides a workspace so this room can serve multiple purposes.

Simple shades are all that is needed for this space.

Magazines and books are great sources of inspiration, so use them to find some ideas and build a game plan, so you don't fly around blindly. If you have time, go to the library and bookstore and just take a quick look. The kids can be entertained with books for them, while you are doing research on the fly!

The whole mantra, "I will know it when I see it," doesn't always apply in design and home decor. You need to be armed with a game plan, because this is a mission. You do not want to stand in the store staring at the same panel for thirty minutes, trying to remember if this color will work. Yes, I have done this, though it occurred prior to my child being mobile, so it wasn't as frustrating.

Consider the room. The family room itself is more of a busy hub of activity and may work better with roman shades versus long panels. If you have a long-haired cat as a resident, you may not want her lying on your drapes. These are things to consider.

It really depends on the style of the window, too. Again research this type of room and look for window ideas so you have a plan. Look at the length. Buying window treatments that just barely touch the bottom of the window sill can often look as if someone came by with a pair of scissors, so keep this in mind. This look works in some spaces, but not all.

When going for a lot of color in the furniture, try to stay neutral on the walls.

A GOOD PAINT JOB

The furniture is arranged, the pillows are on the sofa. Now let's talk about some wall color. Some designers prefer to select a color and then create the space around the room; however, if you are like most, you have been transferring furniture from one residence to the next and you have to work with some pieces that you currently have.

A paint fan will cut down on multiple trips to the store to collect paint swatches.

TIP

A dark wall color works in a large space when paired with white.

The warm gold wall color contrasts nicely with the ottoman and the foyer color is reiterated in the painting and rug.

Like most of us, you probably already have a few things that you have inherited along the way. If you have artwork that you love, then that is a good place to start looking for colors for your space. It is much easier to work by choosing a color from your current furnishings, than painting the wall and trying to work around the color.

When it comes to paint swatches, you can bring them home by the dozens or you can go to your local paint store and purchase a paint fan. This will cut down on running to the store to find more swatches, and you will have it ready when you need to select a color. Since most hardware stores match paint to any swatch, you don't have to worry about the color being discontinued. Paint fans are available at paint suppliers and almost anyone who sells paint can mix any color you choose.

TIP

Remember always to select your paint color in the space you are going to paint, because colors can change dramatically in different lighting. If you are not confident about your color selection, then have a sample made up and do a test before buying all your paint.

Colors play an important role in setting our moods. Remember, the family room is a space where you want to relax, so try to steer clear of something that is so dark that, over time, it will feel like you are in a dungeon, or so bright that you feel electrified every time you walk into the space. Dark colors can work, but they need to be offset by white and lots of light in a large space. Soothing colors work well in any space. If you want to be vibrant, do so with accessories or an accent wall. If you have a favorite color, go up a few shades on the color scale and opt for a softer tone.

TIP

Keys to Painting

- *Opt for a paint that has the primer mixed in, this will go on more smoothly and cover better.*
- *I personally like to use the small sponge rollers. They have a smoother nap for walls and roll faster.*
- *Around trim, floors, or ceilings, either tape or use an edger. If you're good, then do the edges with a chiseled brush.*
- *Make sure you have drop cloths. Old sheets or plastic also work well, especially if you are going to have a small assistant.*

TIP

Suggestions for Paint Finishes

- *Walls: satin or eggshell finish*
- *Trim and doors: semi-gloss finish*
- *Ceilings or walls with imperfections: flat finish*

Soft colors such as grays, off whites, and light blues and greens can make a space appear larger. Accenting the trim with white or ivory exudes a fresh look. For a different look, try colored trim a few shades lighter than the wall shade. This works well in powder rooms and smaller bathrooms.

When painting an open space floor plan, such as a family room opening up to the kitchen, make sure the colors flow well. You will need a little accent of the kitchen color in the family room and vice versa to tie the spaces together.

Remember it is only paint. It isn't that expensive and if you decide you hate it, you can always repaint. Paint is not permanent.

So how do you paint when you're short on time? The quick answer is in steps. If you have your tools ready for the job, your child's snack or nap time is the best time to work on this type of project a little at a time. If it just becomes impossible to work with your little helper around, you may have to hold off until you have someone to keep your little one entertained, and work on something else.

No kids but short on time? In that case, taking it in steps applies to you as well. Move all the furniture to the center of the room or, at least, away from the wall you are working on. Tape off the trim or, if you're good, use a new paint brush with a sharp edge for cutting in and skip the taping. You don't have to do everything in one day, besides your back will probably dislike you for it anyway. Paint a wall at a time if you have to. Remember to take it in steps and you can squeeze a little design in here and there.

When rolling paint on the wall, make sure you do not let paint drip. Roll the paint out completely to prevent dark spots of paint from drying on your wall.

TIP

Once you start, finish the project. Do not leave it unfinished. Set your mind to be done with the job. That is the key to effectively decorating in a quick and efficient manner.

TIP

Need it Now

Paint the inside of a bookcase or built-in for a pop of extra color or paper it with bold printed wallpaper. This only takes about an hour or two for instant gratification (depending on the size of the piece of course!).

LET THERE BE LIGHTING!

The right lighting sets the tone for the space. A lot of homes are equipped with direct lighting overhead, placed in the center of the ceiling, whether it is a ceiling fan with a light or a plain fixture. Some homes have no lighting in the center of the room and may have a switch that controls an outlet into which you plug your lamps.

Indirect lighting is achieved by using table lamps and, in some cases, recessed fixtures, eyeballs, or tracks to create a warm and inviting atmosphere in any space. An overhead light by itself can create harsh lighting in a room. If the space is not to be used for doing tasks, then the warmth of the lamp lighting can create ambience.

A good rule of thumb for placing lamps is to have them beside furniture that is used the most, such as sofas and chairs. If you have a space in the room that appears to be dark, then add a lamp.

It can be a little tricky to achieve the right look with lamps. Make sure you buy a lamp that is large enough for your space so it will not appear lost in the room. You will most likely need two or three for a good balance.

Lighting needs to fill the space.

TIP

Need it Now

Who doesn't love a chandelier? Okay yes I'm sure that a sparkling chandelier isn't the first thing on a guy's mind when working on a room, but if you need an extra touch of lighting and there is no overhead fixture in your bedroom, small office, or other space, a chandelier can be wired to be plugged into an outlet. They also sell this type of pre-wired fixture in many home decor stores. Sometimes it is just the touch you need. If it has a chrome or brass finish, spray paint can change the look to any color you want.

Wallpaper creates a focal point and limits the need for much more treatment.

Time Crunch Family and Living Room

GOT AN HOUR?

- Move throw pillows from another room to the living room, if colors work together.
- Add a slipcover to a worn sofa.
- Arrange the TV, DVD, and DVR remotes in a nice container that compliments your room. A small basket works as well.
- Add a pair of panels to the windows. If they are ready-made, make sure they are ironed first.
- Arrange and hang artwork over the sofa or another major piece in your space.
- Replace an outdated light fixture.
- Teach the kids how to stow away easily accessible toys into baskets and keep them close by.
- If you have climbers in your house, secure all furniture over two feet tall with furniture wall straps!

GOT A COUPLE OF HOURS?

- Put up a display shelf.
- Prep the room for a new coat of paint.
- Buy a new throw rug.
- Rearrange a room.
- Arrange displays on bookshelves or atop another flat surface. Keep them high enough to be above little hands if you have toddlers.

GOT A WEEKEND?

- Select a new color and paint the family or living room. Remember that a color fan is easier to access than several swatches of paint.
- Recover a side chair cushion in a spunky print.
- Clean out clutter and old pieces that just drag the room down and need to go; donate them to your local charity. If dad has a favorite worn out chair, you may have to bend a little on this one or move him, a TV, and a heater to the garage!

Top and bottom Artwork in similar frames displayed across a window sill is an easy way to add pattern to a space without drilling into the walls.

Color in the pillows is reflected in the centerpiece on the coffee table.

4

Is that the
Dinner Burning?
Kitchen
Areas

When going for a theme, try not to overdo it. Instead, add a few pieces here and there such as this porcelain rooster.

The kitchen is one of the most used spaces in the home and for those of us who do not care for cooking, either design inspiration or divine intervention is sometimes needed to make this space work effectively. There's a lot more to a kitchen today than there once was. No longer is the kitchen there just to house a fridge, oven, and dishwasher, hidden away from the rest of the house. It is the center of the home. It needs to work for you and to look good. Homework is done, crafts are made, and stories are told in this space, because it is another important gathering place in the home. The old sentiment is true, no matter if it's a fine dinner party or a gathering of friends; everyone ends up in the kitchen.

A classic kitchen design is always timeless.

Classic design is important in this space. A complete redo may not be in the budget at this time, but a few simple changes can make a great impact in this room. Try to stay away from the theme kitchen. If you have a border over your cabinets in a particular theme, a fresh paint job will bring your kitchen up to date. I know the border with the little fat chef was cute at the time, but it is dated as easily as the wine border, the cow border, the pig border, and so forth and so on. You get the picture!

The kitchen needs to flow with rooms that are connected, so let's not opt for the Big Bird yellow kitchen against the tan family room. It just isn't a good combination. It looks like mustard and mud, and that isn't a good look.

There are a few quick updates that will give you a lot of bang for your buck. Something as simple as accessorizing can make a huge impact on your kitchen, whether it is new dish towels, canisters, or bowls. It may not seem like a huge change, but when you tie them all together the colorful details can make a difference.

If you have oak or another type of wood cabinets, you may simply need to clean them really well and add new hardware. Remember to measure the distance between the drill holes when replacing handles. If you want to opt for knobs then it is possible to fill the remaining drill hole with wood putty and hit it with some stain, but you will be able to see a

A desk in the kitchen provides a place to pay bills and add memos and reminders. Breakables are displayed above, behind the glass doors.

Pots displayed above the island are within easy reach. They also add color and free up space under cabinets.

trace of the hole left behind. Opting to paint the cabinets a fresh white or bisque will also make a huge impact on the space. If going this route, make sure you prep your cabinets and do some research. You want to ensure that the paint does not chip away after all your hard work.

Glass doors in a kitchen allow for a break in the wood as well as a showcase for dishes. A subway tile backsplash always makes for a classic and clean look.

Adding glass doors to your kitchen cabinets can be another way to give character to this space. Frosted or opaque glass will hide less than perfect displays. Have a professional to do this for you.

Adding a backsplash, whether it's colorful mosaics or a simple subway tile, can make a dramatic difference in the kitchen. This is something you could most likely do yourself in a day or two, depending on the size of the wall above your counters.

Love the look of stainless, but not in the budget? A quick way to get the look is by using stainless appliance fronts. These can be found on the web and come in both adhesive and magnetic form.

Three simple pendants over this kitchen island tie the whole space together.

Lighting is another important element in the kitchen. Adequate lighting is necessary in this space, because the kitchen is a task-driven area. You may opt for hanging pendants over an island or bar, with under-cabinet lighting to provide additional countertop light.

Different types of lighting give you more control over the feel of the environment. If it's all hands on deck, then the recessed lighting, pendants, and under cabinet lighting may be needed. For a more relaxed atmosphere, the shift to only under cabinet lighting can completely change the mood.

There are several interesting fixtures available on the market. One is a pendant light that can work with an existing recessed light. They fit into your existing recessed casing much like a light bulb. Nickel goes with most

Add a pretty bouquet of cut flowers for a quick kitchen pick-me-up.

A butcher block countertop contrasts well with these painted white cabinets. The kids artwork, such as the plate in the corner, gives added interest.

Mosaic tiles in one small area, such as above the stove, are quick to put up and make an impact on the kitchen's overall design.

any style, whereas the oil-rubbed bronze or wrought iron is a bit more of an eclectic or traditional mix.

Other lighting options include chandeliers and island fixtures that double as pot holders. Kitchen lighting makes a statement, so be careful in your choices and, as always, research before you go so you are not standing in the hardware store staring at the ceiling in the lighting department for a long period of time. You are sure to be asked at least five times "Why you are staring at the ceiling, mommy ?" To be less frustrated, check the store's website for available options in your area. If you are short on time, you can order online then pick it up at the store.

Time Crunch Kitchen

GOT AN HOUR?

- Clean out the junk drawer.
- Discard old sippy cups if your child has outgrown them, and replace worn utensils.
- Arrange cooking utensils in a pretty container on the counter for easy access.
- Add a pretty bouquet of flowers, whether cut from the yard during blooming season or faux (they last longer!).
- Add a colorful throw rug in front of the sink.

GOT TWO HOURS?

- Replace tired cabinet pulls with nickel, oil-rubbed bronze, or another more up-to-date finish. If you are replacing handles, make sure you measure the distance between the drilled holes to ensure new pulls will fit.
- Arrange a collection of pottery or tin ware above the cabinets if space allows.
- Create a display of china or pottery where glass shelves are. White dishes always make a statement.

GOT A WEEKEND?

- Stain or paint your kitchen island in a contrasting color to the cabinets.
- Replace an old valance with either a new one tied off with ribbons or a wood blind or shade.
- Replace worn out tile in the kitchen with a fresh and new pattern.
- Add stainless steel fronts to your appliances. These can be found online.

Striking displays of collectibles, including china, can be housed in a cabinet with glass doors to show them off as well as prevent dust from collecting.

5

Shall We Dine?
Dining Rooms

Color drives the whole scheme and hanging the drapes higher than the window frame elongates the windows.

Display favorite things on a buffet or sideboard. A pair of topiaries creates a formal look.

*J*ust like a fine dinner, the dining room is one of the spaces where options are endless. Most of our best memories are often created around the table. Who doesn't like to eat? Take inspiration from your furniture when deciding upon a color scheme. This is where you can create an intimate atmosphere and showcase your favorite things, whether it is in a hutch or china cabinet, or atop a buffet. If you prefer to have your table set, then by all means show off the wedding china or grandmother's antiques. You may have to do a little light dusting before having a meal, but it's worth it. If you have little ones running around, save this idea for when they are a bit older.

Whether your idea of a beautiful space is glamorous, modern, or traditional, there are a few key tips in creating the perfect dining space. Some designers prefer to select a color and then create the space around your room; however, if you are like most, you have been dragging furniture from one residence to another and you have to work with what you have. There is a bit of nostalgia attached to what you currently have, after all, and there probably isn't a price tag on that six leaf dining table your mother finally passed down to you. If you want to spice it up a bit, the dining chairs are the place to show some creativity.

The color palette can create an intimate setting, and windows in this space can be made to appear more grand by hanging panels above the window an inch or two, if space allows. The dining table is the main attraction in this space and the color of wood will help you in determining what works best for wall and accent colors. Remember always to work around the main piece. Everything else will unfold naturally.

Personality can be infused in this space with patterned chair cushions. These are pretty easy to reupholster. A yard or less of fabric should do the trick, depending on the size of your chair. Remove the seats, lay the cushion face down on the fabric's unprinted side and fold over the back of the cushion. You need about an inch or two overlap onto the base. Secure with a staple gun.

Lighting makes all the difference. A simple change from an outdated fixture to something new can give your space a whole new look. Add shades to bare bulbs on chandeliers for additional color.

Lighting is so important in the dining room. Most dining rooms are equipped with a large overhead light. Depending on your formality, you may choose a large chandelier or a more modern fixture. Additional lighting can be provided with a pair of lamps on a chest or buffet.

TIP

Need to add some color but a new fixture isn't in the budget? An existing brass chandelier can be spray painted to give the space an entirely different feel. Out with the golden octopus! Magnetic prisms can be added to provide an extra touch of glamour.

A china cabinet provides a place to display treasured collectibles.

Accessories are a key ingredient for adding personality to any space and the dining room is no exception. Don't forget the artwork and the table's centerpiece. This is also a great place to showcase your china on the walls, whether you have little ones or not.

Speaking of china, don't hide it away under the bed, where no one can see it, just because you have little tykes in your home. A cabinet with glass doors is a valuable piece for showing off your best wares in the dining space. If you have an issue with children opening the doors,

Built-ins provide an extra spot for displays and storage. Remember to go up when you run out of space on the floor.

Display plates on the wall in odd numbers to showcase china and add color. This also makes for quick and simple wall art.

then tie a large ribbon around the entire cabinet with a knotted bow on the front. Actually this is a cute idea and keeps little hands out! For the most curious, you may need to add a lock around the knobs and then tie the ribbon so it covers the lock.

Once again make sure your cabinet is securely anchored to the wall so there is no chance junior is going to attempt to scale this piece of furniture.

Need it Now

TIP

A bold arrangement of colorful flowers in a glass vase can add visual interest. Select about five large flowers in a color that contrasts with the room's wall color.

A centerpiece is a must on a dining table; otherwise it looks pretty barren. When deciding upon the centerpiece, the dimensions of the table need to be taken into account, so the decoration does not look lost in the space. Don't be too formal, as you can layer pieces to give height. For example, a cake plate may be just the extra height a short arrangement may need to give it the correct look.

Go faux. I know there was a time when we were told by designers worldwide that faux flowers were a no-no, but if you've got kids or there's not a flower cart parked at the corner of your street, chances are faux is the way to go. They last longer, they look better these days, and you don't have to change them every few days once the petals start falling on your table.

Go with your gut, if you stand back and look at your design or arrangement, and it doesn't seem quite right, chances are it probably isn't.

TIP

A neutral area rug breaks up the space between the wood furniture and wood floor.

Lastly, the floor may need some attention. An area rug warms and softens the floor while anchoring the table. Depending upon your space, you can go pattern or plain. A simple indoor/outdoor rug can reinforce the casual look in an otherwise formal room.

Time Crunch Foyers

GOT AN HOUR?

- Hang three pieces of your best china from smallest to largest in a vertical pattern on a wall in the dining room; add a pretty ribbon behind them for a feminine touch.
- Arrange several flowers in a large vase. Buy a grouping of single-stemmed flowers from your local craft store. Remember odd numbers, between 3 and 5, make a nice grouping.
- Arrange a still life display of your favorite items over the top of your hutch or china cabinet.

GOT TWO HOURS?

- Buy a bold print fabric to recover tired or boring dining chair cushions.
- Paint a worn brass chandelier a bright white for a fresh pop of color.
- Create a large display of plates on the wall. Again, use the top of the table to lay out your design before hitting the wall, because they're breakable and you don't want the kids using them for Frisbees.

GOT A WEEKEND?

- Add chair rail and wainscoting to the dining room.
- Paint the dining room a new color. Chocolates, reds, and terra-cotta are some of my favorites, if they coincide with adjacent rooms.
- Recover the dining chair cushions.

A mirrored chest beside the bed opens up the space by reflecting light. As pretty as this is, you may need to keep the glass cleaner handy if you have toddlers!

6

Restful Retreats: Is There Such a Thing?
Bedrooms

$\mathcal{I}$ am a firm believer that the bedroom should be a restful haven away from the hectic schedule that often controls our lives. We are so busy with work, getting the kids to school, and making dinner, that we need a special place to escape to when the day is over, and a peaceful place to wake up and start the next day. This isn't always realistic when you're a mom of small children; however, simple things such as paint color and linens can create a calming mood for your space, even though a little one is screaming for breakfast first thing in the morning.

When furnishing your bedroom, take into consideration pieces that you already have on hand. The bedroom is made up of a few key pieces in most spaces, such as a bed, dresser and night stands. The dresser needs to have a mirror over it for quick checks out the door and to open up the space by reflecting light. A few prized possessions may make a nice display on the dresser and are away from little hands. A photograph or two, nicely arranged, make a simple display.

The main focal point in this space is the bed. This is where the eye goes as soon as you walk in the room. So let's talk about the bed for a bit. Make it look inviting, yet easy to make up. There are several options available should you not have a complete bedding ensemble. Bed frames are quite inexpensive and allow you the freedom of adding more color and texture to your headboard.

A new discovery I made recently is the inflatable headboard, which is available on-line. Installed in ten minutes, it has the same appearance as a covered headboard and gives instant gratification. These work great in guest rooms and they're pretty inexpensive. Have no fear, they have a slip cover and it does not look like a large pool float! These would work great when you need something in a hurry.

Another option is the covered headboard, which is very popular in decorating magazines and books alike. It can be made from MDF board purchased at hardware stores, cut to size, and covered in batting and fabric stapled to the back of the board. Simple rectangular shapes can be cut to size for you at most hardware stores. Finished headboards can also be

purchased, whether online or at a custom design store. Covered headboards can handle a bold print or use an understated neutral fabric. Select a color that contrasts with your wall color for more impact. Go for a pattern to add definition to the space. If you are unsure of the color, a neutral tone, even if it's a print, can work with most any color scheme.

Headboard wall decals can also be put up in a flash. They can be found online. The children will probably want to help with this project because the decal resembles a big sticker! You will need to take care of the first few steps, but once the decal is on the wall, they can help with smoothing out some of the wrinkles.

TIP

Need it Now

Grab a headboard decal and have it up on the wall in no time. Find them at craft stores and online at www.etsy.com.

Monogrammed bed linens are always a nice touch and add a bit of elegance to any space.

DRESS THE BED!

OCD, for me, is an unmade bed. The bed is made, even if the rest of the house looks like a tornado blew through! Something about this one piece in my house makes the rest of the place seem as if the chaos is in order.

Just like you, the bed needs to be dressed in style. Pillows in various sizes and shapes create a luxurious place to fall into at the end of the day. I personally like Euro pillows in lieu of the standard sham; they are large, square, 26" pillows that add visual interest to the bed. Add a sham and other throw pillows, working from largest to smallest towards the front of the bed, and layering them to create depth and texture.

You can't go wrong with white bed linens. They look fresh and go with any color scheme. You can always use bleach if you're worried about stains!

With pillows, decrease the sizes from the headboard to the front with smaller ones in the front.

Less is more but who doesn't love pillows? These pillows are perfect for a pillow fight!

A toile wallpaper background is accented with the same pattern on the fabric headboard. When using a busy pattern, keep the bed linens and accessories simple, because the wallpaper has already done the work!

Neutral bedspreads give you more flexibility with pillow choices. Patterned bed linens are busy and can often overwhelm a room; however, if you prefer a pattern, go solid on the pillows or use larger patterns on the pillow when a smaller print is used on the bedspread. For example: a herringbone print coverlet is accented by using large floral pillows and a solid pillow or two. Patterns are broken up by throwing a solid cover across the foot of the bed to reflect the solid pillow choice.

A covered headboard in a printed fabric makes a statement, especially when balanced with a neutral bedspread. Patterned bed covers can work, but try to avoid the super enormous floral that was a hit a few decades ago. Texture is also important in the bedroom, so try textured pillows in solids in lieu of a smooth cotton pillow.

A starting point for selecting linen colors can be a piece of artwork, a patterned chair, or even a pillow. The colors are already combined for

TIP

This isn't a book about cleaning and housekeeping, but folding the bedspread back while sitting on the bed will save your spread!

The pattern on this headboard is complemented by the solid pillows and white bedspread.

you in these objects. Pull them together to create your bedding scheme and room design.

Now, if you're worried about smudgy hand prints, finger prints and face prints on your white coverlet, then either don't allow eating in the bedroom or stock up on lots of stain remover! White can be bleached, but make sure you spot treat it first!

A night stand with drawers can house extra items such as lotion and tissue out of sight.

This two-toned night stand of dark wood has a white leather overlay, giving it added definition.

Now onto the other pieces in the space. In the bedroom, a side table or night stand is a must for keeping clutter at bay and necessities within reach. This is where you store the clutter, books, tissues, alarm clock, and plug in your phone.

Tables range from the inexpensive to the luxurious. Not only does the table need to be visually pleasing, it must also serve practical needs. You don't have to be limited to matching bedside tables. As a matter of fact, I prefer mine to be different to give the room an asymmetrical look. Any flat surface, whether it is a small table, desk, dresser, or an actual night stand, can serve the purpose.

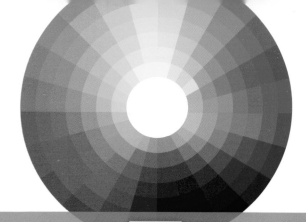

In the guest room, be a little more creative and add a pretty container to house such things as lotion, tissues, or other necessities and make guests feel more at home. Just back it away from the front of the table to keep the queen-of-the-twos from pulling it down!

Bedside tables with a door keep little hands away and provide extra storage. To keep small children out of your things, use a box to house those tiny items. Also, tying a pretty ribbon around a bedstand with a door hides the child lock, increases security, and adds a touch of flare, while keeping kiddos out. Does ribbon seem bit feminine? Then simply add a child lock on the inside of the door. These are very inexpensive and can be picked up at most hardware stores.

The bedside table is also a way to introduce an accent color into the space. Because it is small, a bold color on this type of piece will not be overwhelming.

The easiest and quickest way to paint a small table is with spray paint. Depending upon the size, two to three cans of spray paint over a coat of primer will do the trick. Take the table outside to paint it and let it dry completely between coats. Another trick is to spray paint in a large box in the garage

If you do not have a place that works well for spray painting, then brushing the paint on will work just as well... it just takes a little longer. Make sure you sand the rough edges, prime, and paint. Adding a coat of polyurethane to finish the piece will seal it and limit chipping.

Don't be afraid to have pieces of different finishes in a room. It doesn't have to be matchy- matchy unless that is your preference. Remember there are no hard and fast rules to decorating.

TIP

A Note About Color

We're not going to have a color wheel lesson here, just a review of the basics you need to know to be better equipped to select colors. The simplest way to look at the color wheel is this: if the colors are across from each other, they will work well together. For example, an eggplant sofa in the purple family works well in a green room. I don't recommend the green on the color wheel, so go for something more subdued like celery green. Colors opposite your main color on the wheel work well for accent pieces, accessories, and bedding.

TIP

Need it Now

To assist you with coordinating and contrasting colors, print a color wheel off the internet to keep on hand. In a design scheme, opposite colors almost always work well together.

Always accessorize.

Mirrored furniture reflects light and visually
increases the size of the space.

"Always surround yourself with items you love and bring joy to your life."

Colors play a large role in how we react to our environments. Choose a wall color that relaxes you since that is the goal of this room. My favorite choices are soft greens, lavenders, pastel pinks, coffee colors, and blues. Quite frankly, I think all colors are my favorite!

It's easy to select a color if you purchase your bed linens or accessories first, since they come in far fewer colors them paint does. Once you have bed linens you love, select a paint color that's included in the design of your bed cover, pillows, or even artwork in the room. If, however, you choose the paint color first, a solid white or linen colored bedspread will work. Pick up the colors and add other accents in the pillows.

Once you find a starting point, the design will begin to unfold. Remember, rooms need to flow, so take into consideration adjoining spaces.

Always Accessorize!

Just like an outfit, a room needs accessories, but don't overdo it: too many accessories means more to dust and more to break! Be creative about where to put them, and remember, you can always go up.

Plates hung on the bedroom wall keep them out of reach, but available for all to enjoy, instead of tucked away.

First place them on the bed to get an idea of how they will be placed on the wall. This way they are out of reach while you are trying to figure out the hanging pattern you want to use. Use a level that attaches to the wall for best results when lining up your plates.

Even the smallest change can make a huge impact on a space. Something as simple as a hat from the forties can be used as a lamp decoration. Be sure it doesn't touch the bulb! This little number takes two seconds to throw together and can be done with a pint-size screecher hanging from your pants leg.

Plates can be used in any space to add depth and character to the wall. On the wall it is out of reach! Use a level to ensure they're straight.

THE ESSENCE OF LIGHTING

Lighting is very important in this space as in any other room. Table lamps placed beside the bed provide task lighting and are also a nice decorative accessory. Consider the size of your bedside table when selecting your lamps. Very small, skinny lamps will look lost beside a king-size bed with large night stands.

Lamps need to fit the table, bed, and room proportionally. For example, a very tall and large lamp base will need a larger shade and will be more appropriate for a large room.

A smaller room with a full-size or twin bed is better fitted for a small night stand with a shorter lamp style. If you have lamps passed down from a family member or have scored them at a yard sale, new shades will give them a whole new look. Just make sure everything electrical is in safe, working order.

Some bedrooms have ceiling fans, small overhead lights, or even chandeliers above the bed. If you are in a room with a light that seems dim, change out the bulbs to a higher wattage or go LED. They are more expensive, but the output of light is worth it and they do not get hot, which is a huge plus! No one wants their space to resemble a cheap motel room, so if it's looking a little dim in there, make a change to brighten things up a bit.

Time Crunch Bedrooms

GOT AN HOUR?

- Clean clutter from your bedside table.
- Make the bed and add pillows for color.
- Add a flower arrangement somewhere to give things a feminine touch.
- Add a throw to the end of the bed or a side chair for more color and texture.

GOT TWO HOURS?

- Frame a few photographs of family and friends.
- Arrange artwork to create a focal point above the bed.
- Purchase new lamp shades for tired lamps or new lamps to give the space additional ambience.

GOT A WEEKEND?

- Paint the bedroom a new color that complements existing colors in the space. You may need to have someone watch little tykes for you, but I sometimes paint with my child and let her have a roller and brush. Though this is only recommended for the brave, if you have older kids, they will enjoy helping. Make sure the space is well ventilated!
- Cover a fabric headboard for added texture and pattern. Add covered buttons for additional color.
- Paint a side chair in an accent color and cover the seat cushion with a pretty print for added character. Small chairs can fit most anywhere or in a corner.

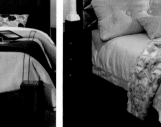

7

*Ahh, The Much
Needed Bubble Bath:*
Bathrooms

Change out a faucet for an easy update.

New hardware breathes new life into existing cabinets.

I once read that a busy mom moved her desk into the bathroom because it was the only place she could be alone! I'm not sure that I can even hide in the bathroom, but since it is most likely the only place to find refuge, indulge yourself with color schemes and finishes that create a relaxing atmosphere. A bathroom makeover can be done with just a few minor changes, such as new paint, a new faucet, and new cabinet hardware.

Cabinet and sink combos give the appearance of furniture in the bathroom and look elegant as well.

Take a look at who uses the bathroom, the size of the room, and what is currently in there. You may be able to paint the cabinets instead of replacing them depending on the style. If you do have to replace them, this isn't nearly as costly as redoing a kitchen. You can opt for a sink and cabinet combo if the space calls for a single sink. The same goes for the powder room.

If a new redo isn't in the budget, simply switch out the lighting, faucet, and hardware. Opt for something up-to-date, such as new knobs or handles in nickel or even glass, depending on your style. These can be found online and in hardware stores. Some craft stores carry a wide variety of hardware in many different colors and styles. A new faucet can add some new life to an outdated bathroom. Got brass? Time to get going!

IMPORTANT TIPS AND TRICKS

Lighting in any room is one of the most important elements to consider when decorating. The bathroom lighting not only needs to be attractive, but also to illuminate the space adequately. For a change of pace consider looking into the outdoor lighting for use indoors. Adding two outdoor lanterns beside a bathroom mirror adds interest and brings the outdoors in.

Lighting comes in an array of colors including cobblestone browns, wrought iron blacks, brushed nickel, brass, and white. If you are looking to make a change, your style will determine the finish that is perfect for your space.

Still sporting the Hollywood bulbs? It's time for an upgrade! The darker finishes work well in traditional spaces and vintage and cottage styles. White and nickel work in cottage and modern decors. If you are eclectic, then break out the spray paint and add a pop of color in a vibrant blue say, or even with an orange chandelier. As you can tell, I have a thing for chandeliers. Bathrooms are another great place to add one. Get a chandelier that is wired to plug into an outlet and hang it from a hook in the ceiling to add extra glamour.

Chandeliers needn't to be saved for formal spaces. This one makes quite a statement over the garden tub in this master bath.

Lighting beside the mirror gives a different look than the standard, above the mirror, vanity light.

An initial on a neutral shower curtain adds a high end touch.

If the walls are neutral, a damask type print works well in a bold color.

A textured white shower curtain works well in almost any bathroom scheme.

Shower curtains are another factor to consider when accessorizing the bathroom. Try to steer away from the busy floral prints, unless it's a bold damask or vibrant color. There are many styles to choose from in ready-made, but if you can't find exactly what you're looking for, go custom. A shower curtain is basically four straight seams, and you can use curtain rings with clips to attach it to the rod. For a higher end look, go for a textured white or cream.

Monograms can be added to shower curtains and towels for an upscale, custom look. If you are unsure of what color to select, go for a monochromatic look. You can never go wrong with an antique white or pure white shower curtain with the monogram in a gray or brown tone. Neutral towels and shower curtains work well in almost any bathroom setting.

A bright green against the white cabinets and flooring is accented nicely with the black and white toile window treatment and black accessories.

Wall color can affect your mood in so many ways and, since this is the hiding place, it is essential to choose one that is either calming or fun, depending on how you want to spend your little tiny bit of "me" time... if there is such a thing! A bathroom can be a bright color, so this is a place where you can introduce a more flashy color on the wall. Wallpaper is also making a comeback. Make sure you select something you will not tire of easily. A powder room is one of the best ways to introduce a bold print in damask or even an animal print. This is most likely a weekend project.

Make the space appear lived in and use furniture when there is enough space. Also, accessorize with some of your favorite pieces. Go ahead and add picture frames and some glassware. The glass pieces can be filled with soaps and bath salts or simply displayed on a shelf or atop a chest, if space allows. Use plastic if they are within the reach of little hands.

Window treatments in this space can range from a Roman shade to a full panel depending on the size of your window. Make sure you have some coverage on the window such as a blind or shade for privacy. Roman shades provide privacy at night and can be raised up as a decorative treatment at other times.

This bathroom built-in stores towels and other necessities, but a photograph or two can also be added for a bit of personality.

Small cabinets that can be placed in the bathroom not only provide much needed space for toiletries but also add a bit of character. This cabinet, which is the same color as the trim, gives the illusion of a built-in.

BATHROOM STORAGE

Small bathrooms, such as powder rooms and bathrooms in older homes, usually lack storage space. And even if you have brand new cabinets, there is often no way everything can fit in the base cabinets. By the way, if you keep cleaning products or anything that could be hazardous to little ones under the sink, make sure there is a child lock on the doors.

There are a few simple ways to create more space in your bathroom. If there is room, extra storage space can be provided with a small, floor standing cabinet with two or three shelves to hold toilet paper and wash cloths. The top of the cabinet can hold soaps in a glass bowl, candy dish or small basket. This makes an attractive and functional addition. When purchasing any piece of furniture, make sure you take the measurements of what can fit in the space and take the measuring tape with you when you go shopping.

If you are out of space to house necessities such as hairbrushes, nail polishes, and other small items, a small basket that fits in the cabinet will keep everything stored in an orderly fashion.

Keep the items you are always using handy in a container on the vanity. Not only will they be within easy reach, but there is less clutter on the counter. This keeps everything organized.

It may take some time to find the perfect storage piece, but antique shops that have multiple vendors are your best places to find unique pieces.

Containers that store Q-tips and cotton balls can also be incorporated as a design element

If space allows, a piece of furniture provides storage for linens and paper products, and a place to display a favorite photograph or two.

TIP

Need it Now

Precut shelves and brackets can be found at hardware stores and hung in about 20 minutes. Opt for the prefinished in white, black, or wood grain types and remember to use a level so you're not watching items fall off into the potty!

More space can be added in the bathroom by adding a couple of shelves over the toilet. This is a space that is often overlooked but with a few extra shelves and some decorative containers you can house extra paper, cosmetics, personal care items, and even cleaning products, freeing up valuable cabinet space.

Above the potty shelving! Filling this forgotten little space with shelving creates an extra nook for toiletries.

Frame or replace a frameless wall mirror.

If the existing tile and grout is in good condition, give a fresh look by bleaching it.

No outfit is complete without DOG HAIRS

Time Crunch Bathrooms

GOT AN HOUR?

- Change out towels to one color. Neutrals and earth tones will balance well with any bathroom color and give it a new and fresh look. You would be amazed by what new towels can do!
- Replace the shower curtain and rod. Lift the curtain about 3 to 4 inches from the floor to add extra height.
- Place a pretty basket on the counter or elsewhere to house soaps and extra hand towels.
- Add greenery for a fresh look.
- Change existing hardware. In a small bathroom go for something fun like glass knobs or colored ones.

GOT TWO HOURS?

- Hang a shelf or two above the toilet and store extras in coordinating baskets or containers.
- Change out your old faucet with a more contemporary one in nickel or oil-rubbed bronze.
- Replace the old mirror with a new one.
- Tape off the walls to get ready to paint a new color.

GOT A WEEKEND?

- Paint the room a soothing color such as a soft green, blue, or an earth tone for a refreshing feel.
- Tear down an old wall-size mirror and replace with a framed mirror or add a frame around an existing glued-on mirror and paint or stain the frame to coordinate with the color scheme.
- Bleach the grout and tile by mixing three parts water to one part bleach.

Add greenery.

If the kids have a separate bathroom that isn't used by others, then go all out in here. They're only little once!

A bold printed wallpaper is toned down with white bed linens.

8

$\mathcal{I}$ must admit, this is my favorite space to design. If I had the means to hire a nanny, I would have more children just so I could design all their rooms! This is such a fun space, where color can pack a punch and it all works together. Although you do have to take into account adjacent rooms, this can be done by using the same color of trim or one similar color from the adjoining space in the room.

Try to avoid the movie themes, because they will outgrow those soon and move on. However, if your little one is insistent upon the idea, you can incorporate a movie-themed pillow or accessories in the space so they can easily be switched once they have decided they are ready for a change.

Toys and books can be incorporated into the design with stylish bookcases, shelves, baskets, and bins.

Color and texture is very important in this space. Children love to snuggle against a minky chenille pillow or a fuzzy blanket. These also add visual interest to the room. It is important to spark creativity in your child, so do it by creating a fun and exciting space where they can sleep and play.

This removable castle tent is incredibly fun and when your princess outgrows this stage, the bed will grow with her for years to come.

Most bedrooms do double duty as both a play space and a sleeping area, so, to keep the chaos low, shelves and bookcases may be needed to store toys. Any extra closet space will work as toy overflow as well.

Most children love to have a small table and chairs where they sit, play, or color. If space allows, try to place one in this room or, if you are fortunate enough, in the play room, which is even better.

Bins under the bed provide storage that is easy for little ones to reach and hides toys out of sight quickly when needed.

Provide a place for homework and play if space allows.

Opt for darker furniture in lieu of dark paint and contrast with a bright wall color.

Toddlers and teenagers will want to have some say in their space. If your teenager asks for a black wall, you may need to make some compromises, perhaps with black accents or black furniture. This way everyone is happy. Try to select a scheme that will flow with coordinating rooms. If every other room connecting to this room is in the neutral scheme, then suddenly having a Kermit-the-frog-green space probably isn't going to flow as well. So maybe opt for a softer green.

Have fun decorating this space. This is the one space that allows you to let loose with your creativity. Add color and texture on the bed through pillows. If you are just unsure of how to get started with your color choices, take inspiration from one of your child's art pieces or even a favorite pillow. Textile designers and artist have already selected the perfect color schemes in their pieces, so find a favorite and began to unfold your perfect design. All you need is a starting point.

Color is the main focus in this room as in any space. In order to involve your child in choosing their paint color, lay out a few colors that you can live with and let them choose from one of those that you like best. For example, if your little princess likes blue, then have four different shades of blue that will work well with adjoining spaces and have her choose from one of those. Not only is she involved in the process but you will have a color that will work with the rest of your space versus having a Crayola® or navy blue room amongst several rooms that are earth tones.

This is a very bright and lively color scheme, so make sure something like this flows with the adjoining room. It needs to be neutral with a hint of blue to tie the spaces together.

Camouflage bedding works in a neutral toned room with earth tones on the wall.

Add a chandelier.

If your teenager's taste is not so pleasant, maybe you could pay them off? Or opt for a compromise. Incorporate their taste in other ways if their paint color choice is unsettling. As stated before, showcase their taste with accessories or bed linens.

Closet space needs to be utilized in every way in children's rooms. When you have babies and toddlers, you may be able to have extra rods due to the shortness of their clothes. This will let you store more. As they get older, the shirts can be hung closer to the floor and longer clothing on the top rod. As time goes by you can simply remove the bottom rod if the clothing begins dragging on the floor. Closet organizers work well and provide extra shelving.

Be creative when adding lighting and other accessories to this space. Your child's artwork can be framed and grouped in odd numbers and hung as an arrangement on the wall. Lighting can range from chandeliers to recessed lights. Lamps also come in an array of different styles for kids' spaces, so purchase some cute ones. After all, they're only small for a short while, so indulge yourself with some super cute bedside lamps.

H

Sawyer James

TIP

Need it Now

If you are running out of time, need a space to put baby, but don't have an extra room, then clean out a walk-in closet completely, including rods and shelves. This only works if the crib will fit. Paint the space a bright color and add a couple of framed artwork pieces on one of the walls where baby cannot pull it down. This works well if you need extra space at Grandma's, are in an apartment, or have a small home. Even a small corner can be dedicated to baby and separated by a folding screen for privacy.

SWEET, SWEET BABY

Babies don't require much when they first come into the world, but I don't know a mother anywhere who doesn't dream of a beautiful nursery! A crib, a glider or rocker, a changing table, or a bed works for this as well if there is room in your space, and a you will really need a chest of drawers or some type of storage unit. Many chests of drawers can work double duty as a changing table with a pad installed on top.

Large wall decals go up in a flash and make an impact in a child's space.

KEEPING BABY SAFE

Once baby is toddling around, there are a few things you have to consider in their room as well as your whole house.

- Install outlet covers,
- Don't leave any electrical cords hanging from furniture and do not run them under rugs,
- Use window treatments without looped cords and keep all cords out of reach,
- If you paint the crib, make sure you install a snap-on crib rail protector. These are plastic and are very inexpensive. They can be found at most general merchandise stores or online.
- Install childproof locks on any cabinet doors that house lotions or anything you don't want baby in that could be harmful.
- If you have access to the attic or any other space baby shouldn't get to, install door knob covers.
- Install a smoke alarm in the room.
- Keep the rails of the crib up when baby is in the crib.
- Remove small objects that baby can swallow.
- Make sure any heavy furniture is secure and cannot topple on the baby if he or she pulls on the front. Anchor anything above two feet tall to the wall with furniture straps found online.
- Follow the consumer product safety commission's recommendations regarding cribs

Shelving is the perfect hideaway where toys can be stowed and within easy reach.

For windows, simple panels that do not have dangerous cords can be easily opened and closed. Roman shades also work well. Just make sure the cord is hooked up high where toddlers cannot access it. You may need to install a small hook beside the window to hang the cord on. Make sure it is out of reach from babies and toddlers! This is very important.

The nursery is such a sweet space and you will most likely just enjoy being in it. You can keep it simple, but children are only small for such a short amount of time that you feel free to go ahead and splurge on something that will make this space unique.

Paint the walls a pretty color. Add panels or another type of window treatment and a pretty rug. Display some of your favorite baby things and maybe even some of your own childhood memories or photos for a bit of nostalgia. A simple wall decal that goes up pretty quickly will make a statement as soon as someone enters the room.

Extra storage in this space can, once again, be found in the way of baskets and wall shelves. Hide diapers, lotions, and other necessities in baskets under a changing table. Extra space can be found under the crib or bed if there is one in the room. Store crib sheets under the crib and seasonal clothing under the bed in containers if you buy ahead. The good thing about babies is that their clothes are small and you can store a lot more in a little space!

Enjoy this stage, because as we all know, it doesn't last long and soon they will be cruising all over the house and on a mission to destroy!

Add texture in pillows
and throws.

Add personal touches such as
photographs in similar frames.

101

GOT AN HOUR?

- Frame three to five of your child's best artwork in black or white coordinating frames.
- Print several candid shots of your children and their friends and put them in 4x6 and 5x7 frames to display.
- Order new bedding. Make sure you measure the distance between the bed and floor for bed skirts to ensure you have the correct drop length. A short skirt looks silly, as if someone came by and cut the length.
- Change hardware on a piece of furniture to a colorful handle or knob.

GOT TWO HOURS?

- Rearrange the bedroom.
- Organize the toys in colored cubes to get them off the floor.
- Hang a new light fixture that has some personality. Light fixtures are often overlooked, but a simple change can breathe new life into a space. Remember, this one can be fun!
- Add a new window treatment. Make sure you measure for the accurate length before buying. Buying online helps with keeping your sanity!

GOT A WEEKEND?

- Score a vintage dresser at a yard sale and paint it pink, blue, or some other fun color. Remember to prep before painting and apply a sealer when you are finished to seal paint. Paints with primers are quicker to use and cover better.
- Paint an outdated room a new color.
- Paint the trim a crisp white or cream.

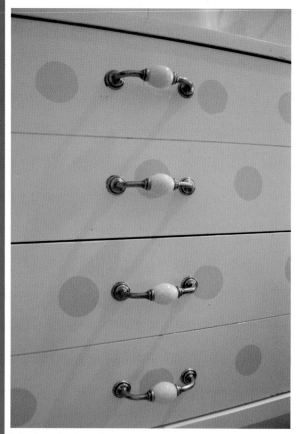

Polka dots painted on a vintage dresser and livened up with new hardware fit just right in a child's room and is quickly done with templates.

9

Beware of
Falling Objects!
Playrooms
and
Workrooms

A horse and rider cut out of wallpaper adds an interesting dynamic to this wall space.

*J*f you are fortunate enough to have a space to house toys, crafts, and other hobbies, then you are living the life! These areas can be combined to ensure the best use of the space is achieved with shelves and racks for toys, a desk and tables for crafts, as well as plenty of storage to keep the trip hazards at bay! Color is as important in this room as any other, because, in order to perform at your best, you need to feel comfortable and inspired. If you are like most moms who work from home, peace isn't common, so install ear buds and crank up the iPod, and let the kids run amuck... with some limitations of course!

Tuck away books and stuffed pets in cubby-style bookcases that are easy to assemble.

TIP
Need it Now

If you are in a hurry, as most women are, metal shelving racks can be assembled and up for storage in 30 minutes or less. Add baskets or fabric boxes on the shelves and voilà! Instant storage for the toys! Anchor shelves to the wall with furniture straps found online, to prevent falling on small tots. Designate the top for mom's storage and the bottom for the kiddos.

PLAYROOMS

Who doesn't love to play? Playing needs space, so, if you have a spare room for a playroom or even a small space under the stairs, your kids will appreciate it. A basic playroom needs a bright color for personality, a good storage system, and room to play.

An under-the-stairs play space, which we refer to as the cubby hole at our home, is a perfect spot for a toddler up to preschool age to play and be near the activity going on in the kitchen. Children do like a small space and they like to be near their parents. This space is used a lot, so, of course, it doesn't always look tidy, but it only takes a few moments to reorganize. Originally a closet, a bright color was added to the walls and there is enough room for a couple of bookcases, a small chair and some books to create a reading nook. Two little ones can play in it comfortably.

Toys are hid away in coordinated baskets and a chalkboard for creativity is on the opposite wall. If it's too messy, we close the door, which helps with clutter in the living area.

The space under the stairs makes a nice play place and, because it is close to the adults in the home, kids are more likely to play there.

Kids can easily clean up using small baskets meant for each toy. I could have opted for the fancy toys that look like no one plays with them, but this is reality!

Like I said before, this isn't a book on organizing, but clutter of extra clothes and toys needs to go. Clutter in the house will eventually clutter your mind. Old toys that aren't played with as much can be donated or sold to make room for new.

Rotate toys out of the space so your kids will feel as if they have new ones. This cuts down on the amount of toys in the room at any given time.

A storage system will keep toys off the floor as well as add visual interest to the space. Colored containers can be designated as pink for crayons, blue for cars, and so forth, if you're going all out with color. If you're trying to make it appear as a predominately grown-up space, neutral baskets will do the trick. Baskets and containers need to coordinate with the colors of the space to ensure the room looks cohesive.

A good play area needs a table and chairs, preferably kid size, bookshelves for books and toys, and a small chair for reading. Book shelves and built-ins will give you the most storage. The small cubby storage units found at most retailers work very well in a play area to corral toys, puzzles, and coloring books. For out of reach storage, a step stool that is appropriate for kids is a must. Make sure it is a stool that will not turn over and is meant for children. Children are accident prone as it is, so let's not increase it with an inappropriate step stool!

When it comes to wall color, this space is much like the children's rooms. You can breathe so much personality into this space. So select a fun color or wallpaper and have the kids help you. Remember, don't give them the entire paint fan, but rather select three good colors that you are considering and

A small book shelf can fit in most any space.

have them choose one. If this space will be doubling as a work space as well, give careful consideration to the color choices. A soft khaki or kiwi green can make the space work for both activities. The adult side can be more grown-up, while the playroom side will have a little fun by adding large animal or tree decals to the walls. Many can be found on www.etsy.com and they can easily be put up, then removed when your children either outgrow this space or it is transformed into something different.

Colorful fabric boxes not only hide toys, but also tie the room's overall design together. Choose colors that match your theme.

Wall decals and kid's artwork can be used to adorn the walls.

A table for playing, coloring, and, of course, fine dining is a good idea for any play space.

AND THE EXTRAS!

As in any area of the home, lighting plays an important role. There are so many lighting choices in interesting combinations available today. This space doesn't necessarily need to create a certain ambience since this is a task driven space, but it can allow you to choose something a little outside of your normal comfort zone when it comes to design. This is the area where you can unleash your inner child. This is probably why my favorite spaces to design revolve around children. But don't be tacky! Make sure you have enough lighting through overhead lights and also task lighting at your work area if this is doubling as an office. Recessed lighting is also good for showcasing specific areas in the room, such as artwork or the desk area, and provides a nice ambience.

Frame a drawing or two of your child's artwork for added interest.

When it comes to artwork, the playroom is where you can showcase all the crafts from preschool and Kindergarten! Frame several of your child's best artwork in white frames and hang them on the wall in groups of three, six, or even nine. A fabric covered pinboard can also showcase favorite pieces of their best work, as well as cards from grandma and the most adoring aunt. Rotate pieces out when new projects come through. They are so proud of their artwork and this can cut down on the refrigerator's clutter.

A colorful pinboard provides a place for coloring book pictures and cards.

Hooks provide a place to hang backpacks, hats, and dress up clothes.

WORKROOMS

Assuming Work Can Be Accomplished Around Kids!

A large playroom can also work as a workroom for mom or dad if there is enough room to create a division of space. When noise is a problem where the kids are playing, and it will be, insert your ear buds. Chances are you will probably get more done if they are in the same space busy with an activity. Now if you have a lot of kids, well the best bet is to just hide somewhere if you want to get anything done!

A unit that fits in the corner of a play area doubles as an office. Keep the doors locked if you've got investigative toddlers and preschoolers.

Hooray for built-ins! A small wall that can house a built-in, does double duty as an office and place for treasured items.

A spare room can multi task if the space is used wisely. This is where built-ins work wonders if they are in the budget. They can provide so much more space because things are off the floor. If you are going this route, have a professional assist you with this to ensure you get the best use of space.

Part of the room can be allocated for play, with the other part serving as an office or work area, whether this is crafts, home business, or sewing. Basically it is an area where you, as an adult, can be while the kids are in the room playing, especially smaller ones that need to be supervised. The key to getting any work done with kids is to keep them busy!

One option which has been popular for quite some time is closets converted into offices. There are a multitude of things you can do with space. The key is using your imagination and de-cluttering. De-cluttering is the key

to keeping a space both usable and attractive. When the children outgrow their toys donate them and let them have a hand in helping select which ones need to go. They are sometimes more likely to help with the process and give up their toys if they know they are helping someone else. Of course, in my case this has to be done when the little boss is not home. There is some truth to the phrase, out of sight out of mind.

For a playroom that is also doubling as a work area, make sure that you have important papers locked away or behind doors that the kids will not be able to get into. You may need to add a lock or keep everything of importance that you don't want strewn across the room in the upper part of the desk. If your desk doesn't have a credenza-type piece, then hang a shelf or two above the desk to house important items in containers.

Use a wall unit on a spare wall as the office area. The play area can be in the remainder of the room.

Time Crunch Playrooms and Workrooms

GOT AN HOUR?

- Frame a grouping of three or more pieces of your child's favorite artwork to display.
- Assemble a prefab book case that holds containers for toys.
- Add wall hooks to hang everything from backpacks to dress-up clothes.
- Purchase a bright colored rug online.

GOT TWO HOURS?

- Organize desk or work space efficiently so papers are together and within easy reach.
- Hang a shelf over your desk.
- Organize toys in fabric bins, also called fabric drawers, or baskets. Make sure you measure the space you are buying the baskets for to ensure an accurate fit!

GOT A WEEKEND?

- Construct a custom built-in for toys.
- Paint the playroom a bright and fun color.
- Paint a smooth ceiling a soft blue.

A wooden shutter provides a simple and quick command center and houses the keys.

Black-and-white photographs framed in black frames with white mats always make for a striking display.

10

Up, Up, and Away!
Displays

Display the china!

Collections are what make us unique. I started collecting as a small child because my grandmother would not buy me toys; instead she would buy something I could keep or collect. Well, I guess that is where it all started! My grandpa, on the other hand, did supply my need for Barbies!

Whether we began collecting as a kid or have just started, most of us are proud of our collections and so we need a place to display our treasures. Maybe you have heirloom china or a favorite painting you've carried with you from place to place. When children come into our lives, it does adjust the way we think about things, including our design spaces; but there is no reason you can't have it all.

So instead of packing away all the beautiful collections you have so treasured, look to the walls and start going up. As long as they are out of reach, there's no reason they can't be on display. As a matter of fact, the higher they are on the wall, the less likely you will see dust, so it even cuts down on cleaning!

Built-ins provide places for displaying books and collectibles, and can store unused items underneath. They also add character to a space.

Adding bookcases for height creates visual interest in a display.

Built-ins are my absolute favorite hard-working pieces. I would probably swath my house in built-ins if the budget allowed. Not only are they fabulous for displaying items you want out of reach of little hands, but you can stow away excess items underneath and they can make the smallest space useful.

However, all houses are not equipped with these lovely additions. Several options include assemble-it-yourself bookcases found at mass merchants and stock cabinets found at the hardware store. They can be painted any color and cabinets can be locked to keep curious little ones out. Another option is a media center to house the TV and its equipment, and display favorite items as well. Just because you have children, your house does not have to resemble a day care center!

Believe me, I know that carrying on a conversation consisting of 50 questions on why the sky is blue can take the wind out of your sails, but just because you have little ones does not prevent your home from being a well-designed space. I usually scoffed when people told me that my home would never look the same after having a child. Well, I will admit that they were right. It actually looks better, because I had to be more creative in how I displayed artwork and other collections and I had to think about what would work well in a space and be functional instead of just pretty. It made me think more about the design and, in turn, caused me to create a better space that was both more functional and much more appealing aesthetically.

So let's get into the meat of displaying favorite pieces. Try to incorporate one piece that can work as a place for the electronics and displays at the same time, especially if you are lacking space. One piece that multi-tasks can work wonders for a room such as a family room or multi-purpose room.

You can create the same look with preassembled bookcases. Paint them the same color as your trim and they will look like built-ins. Make sure they are secured on the back to insure they do not topple over on the tots. This is something to consider with anything with weight to it which has a knob or a place for a foot to catch on and climb. Safety is most important when dealing with little ones. All children aren't climbers, but if you have one in your house, take the safety precautions!

If budget allows, a built-in can be customized to your space. Unless you are very handy with carpentry tools, it is best to have someone like a contractor or skilled carpenter view the space in which you are considering adding the built-in, so it will fit precisely. It may be a bit more expensive then a pre-made built-in, but, if space and budget allow, it is worth the end result.

If there is a space in your home that is unused, such as the end of a hallway or what is considered a dead space in a living room or other room in your home, then consider having one made or take it on as a DIY project, because it will turn a useless space into a hardworking one. Everyone needs more space, so look at places you wouldn't otherwise consider! Another option is shelving. A number of shelves stacked will also allow you to use the wall space and keep clutter off the floor.

When considering the display of pieces, a good rule of thumb is to group them in odd numbers. Any type of unit that has shelving can provide space for pottery, glass, and other breakables.

Three is a good number. This type of display doesn't require extensive planning and can be up in no time.

TIP

Need it Now

Metal shelving racks, which are often used in industrial or kitchen spaces, create a modern display for everything from photos to recipe books. Storage can be provided with collapsible boxes in colors coordinated to your scheme. Remember to anchor to the wall to prevent them from tipping over on little ones.

Freestanding storage is another option; this includes everything from shelf units to armoires. Towels in a bathroom can be stored on a small shelf unit, along with toiletries. A shelf unit can double as a TV stand and provide storage for equipment or boxes and baskets for toys.

A simple cabinet like this can be placed in most any space.

Collectibles are accented in a
lighted display cabinet.

In the dining room, storage pieces can include china cabinets, servers, and buffets. This of course is where you can store your china, but it doesn't have to be quite so formal if you add a few pieces of pottery or artwork into the cabinet. Buffets are tall enough that whatever is displayed on top is usually out of the reach of the tot crowd.

A bedroom armoire provides extra storage for out of season bedding. Toys can be hidden in here too!

If a group of art has matching pieces, such as these four, buy them all and you've already done the work of deciding how to hang them.

The list goes on for storage as well as dressers and night stands in the bedroom and multipurpose pieces such as chests. These types of pieces need not be confined to the bedroom, because a dresser can work as a TV stand in a more eclectic setting, providing drawers to house electronics, and a night stand can work as an end table. Good design is acquired over time, but with simple steps you can get to a quicker end result. You will want to allow some room for change from time to time.

So now that the collections are out for all to see, let's work on those walls. Bare walls are like people without clothes. You don't necessarily want to see them!

ARTWORK, YOU SAY?

Artwork should be out for all to see, and it doesn't have to be limited to framed paintings. A stairwell is a great place to showcase a collection of artwork or photographs. Grouping pieces in variously sized frames is appealing as long as the color of the frame is similar. This is where you can display a multitude of photographs, instead of covering the tops of all the furniture with various frames. A hodgepodge of photos in frames completely covering the top of a sofa table appears cluttered.

Frame candid shots and hang them on the wall together in lieu of photo frames grouped in large quantities. Similar frames, such as these black ones, create a more cohesive display.

Be creative when displaying photos and make them part of your home. People will stop and look at them. Take to the walls with the photos and limit the number displayed around your home to a few favorites. Candid shots often make the best artwork. Varying sizes adds interest to the wall in a stair step pattern up the stair well.

Kids' artwork from school is another way to introduce color to your walls. Frame it simply and group several pieces together. This works well in their room or the playroom. It also makes a fun display in a bathroom.

Have your children create artwork by purchasing a canvas or two and let them paint for a particular space, such as a powder room. Have colors set out that coordinate with the space and let them have a part in designing the space. Children love to help and they will get to see their creation every time they go in the room where it is on display.

Children love to assist with whatever project you are doing. Depending on your child, give them a small task to do, because not only will they feel as though they are assisting, it will actually help you to keep them busy. Most children tire of the task after a few minutes anyway and will often move on to something else.

A large painting works well over a large piece of furniture or in a dining space. Added interest can be created by hanging two to three other pieces adjacent to the larger painting by shifting it to the side. This way there is not so much empty wall encasing the piece.

A framed photo, along with books for added height and a lamp, makes an interesting display. Use your photographs sparingly throughout your space.

The I Hate to Housekeep Book
PEG BRACKEN

house beautiful

GREAT STYLE

Slavin
OPULENT TEXTILES

SCREEN GODDESSES

JACKIE O. - A LIFE IN PICTURES

A large clock makes a nice display and you will always know when you're running late! Aren't we all?

A large piece such as a clock or vintage signage creates a focal point and gives the room a certain industrial appeal. These eclectic pieces always make for a striking display. This idea can work in most any design from a minimalist space to a loft or something more traditional.

Black-and-white photos, enlarged to poster size and placed in black frames, are equally appealing in a space like a hallway or over a sofa. Each child's photo enlarged and printed on canvas is an appealing display. Canvas gives the photo the feeling of a painting and appears more like artwork than a photograph while giving off a little bit of a contemporary feel. However, it works just as well in a traditional space. Over a sofa, try the display in a group of three.

Mirrored frames adds dimensionality.

Display favorite things that reflect your little place in the world, such as this nautical theme.

Paintings, photographs, and other artwork can be arranged on several walls. A triangular, square, or rectangular pattern works well on a large expanse of wall. Make sure you take into account the proportions and sizes of your frames. A grouping of pieces is more visually stimulating compared to one or two pieces that are spread far apart on an expanse of wall.

Plates are another favorite of mine. It seems like I had my first set of china by age eight, if that tells you anything! The circular shape of the plates makes a beautiful display and will allow you to showcase some wedding china or other pieces that you want to see but can't allow to be on the table for fear that they will be used as flying discs. Also, a circular piece can add visual interest to a wall otherwise full of squares!

Plate hangers are quite inexpensive and easy to use. I am not a huge fan of plate racks, preferring plate hangers because you can display more in a variety of shapes and sizes on a wall. Again, as before, set them on the floor or a table to get a good idea of how you want to hang them before you start hammering nails in the wall.

Plates do not have to be limited to the dining room and kitchen. They can be showcased over a sofa in the living or family room, as well as over the bed in a guest room.

Look for interesting frames or add ribbon for added aesthetics. Frame your candid shots.

I didn't ask to be Princess
But hey, if the Crown Fits

Keep like colors together to create a more visually pleasing grouping, such as these photos in colors similar to the wall color.

Mirrors are another important piece to consider. A mirror can open up a space and make it appear much larger than it is, a key to a good design. Just so we are clear, I am not condoning mirrored walls that were popular in the eighties. If you already have them you probably have to work with them, but don't add them!

I personally prefer to have at least one mirror in every space. Mirrors are available in every size and shape and various sizes can be grouped and used as a wall display. For a feminine touch, add a ribbon just above a frameless mirror with a small tack nail and stream the ribbon behind the mirror to make it appear as if it is hanging from the ribbon.

TIP

Mark on the wall with pencil before you start drilling and hammering holes in the wall. Do this by holding the plate up to the wall marking just below the top of the plate so you will be able to hang it on the hook. Try various sizes of plates, such as platters, dinner plates, bread plates and saucers, for variety.

Time Crunch Displays

GOT AN HOUR?

- Take an inventory of what you currently have; you may need to move a piece from another space.
- Arrange a display of pottery or another collection in a group of three or five in various sizes on the top of a cabinet or shelf.
- Print several photographs in various sizes that have been hanging out on the computer and have them framed.

GOT TWO HOURS?

- Paint the back of a book shelf or built-in with a contrasting color or add a bold print wallpaper in a damask.
- Assemble a metal shelving unit to house cookbooks, kitchen appliances, and pottery. Make sure it is anchored to the wall if you have children. Their weight can tip the piece over if they are prone to climbing.
- Arrange several photographs to create a wall display.

GOT A WEEKEND?

- Paint a bookshelf or wall unit a fresh color; opting for the same color as the trim creates the look of a built-in and works if you are unsure what color to choose.
- Purge old knickknacks that have lost their luster to make room for a less cluttered look.

Take it up a notch with favorite finds on a shelf.

Take a cue for your room's color scheme from artwork.

Ready-made window treatments, straight from the store shelf, can be up in a no time.

11

Tying It All Together

Something as simple as a change of hardware creates a huge impact in the design of a space and can be done in less than five minutes.

"The smallest changes make the biggest impact."

We've been through the entire house, top to bottom and yet it may seem as if something is missing. It takes a few tweaks here and there to tie the entire space together. Maybe you have blue or burgundy carpeting and just don't quite know what to do to get the space to be visually pleasing. This is typical of older homes, especially if they have been through several different homeowners. I've always thought that it would it be fun to do a family tree of my house. What would these walls say? You may be the homeowner that comes in after someone had an insatiable love for green, with green wallpaper, green carpet, and green tile. Believe me, it's possible. Try to limit the focus on too much color and make the room feel more comfortable by paying careful attention to the right wall color, accessories, and lighting. You can have a beautiful space even with little ones, you just have to move most things up at a higher level and break the process down into steps.

Once you start, commit to the project.

Once you start a project, finish it. Do not leave projects unfinished because you will become overwhelmed and feel like you are living in chaos. When you start to lose interest, just think of the end result.

Good design is acquired over time, but quick and easy steps will help you get the look you desire more quickly. This journey has probably been a tiring one, because you have either crammed every last hour you have left after work into working on your space or you are just tired of hearing your child ask you five times why you are hanging a particular picture on that wall.

Don't give up just yet! There are a few other important items that need to be mentioned that will help make this whole process a little bit easier. The smallest changes make the biggest impact. If you can make only a few of these at first, you will be well on your way toward the beautiful space you desire. Whether it is the perfect sage green lampshade, the chenille pillow, or the prisms hanging from the chandelier, these last few details can bring the space together. Here are a few tips that will make designing on the fly more efficient for you.

How to buy a lampshade

Finding a lampshade without the lamp is sort of like buying a hat without your head. Either take the lamp with you to the store or have a photo of the lamp to use as reference. The lamp store is likely to have other lamps similar to yours in size and shape, so try various shades on a similar lamp. If you've got the nerve, take the kids. Children wearing lampshades makes great pictures for Facebook®!

Try one on for size!

"The more there is, the more there is to dust!"

Accessory selection

Don't be afraid to accessorize, but do not over-accessorize. This happens all too often and creates a cluttered look. If it looks like too much, chances are it is. For example, on a mantle you can either use a large painting or an oversized photograph. Sometimes, mirrors are also used as primary accessories for the mantle or console. Choose smaller items that match your primary accessory and keep them on both sides to create a balanced look. Accent lighting can also be used to highlight the accessories. Remember, the more there is, the more there is to dust!

Color selection

Choose a color from the items you already have. It is easier to paint a room than to buy everything brand new to accommodate a color. Pick up a paint fan to cut down on multiple trips to the hardware store. Pull a color from existing fabric or furniture that will be in the space. Contrasting colors always work, but don't pick sunshine yellow for the family room because you have a navy blue sofa. Go for either butter or a cream if you like yellow.

Item placement

Groupings in odd numbers are usually more visually appealing than those in even numbers; however, this rule does not always apply when hanging artwork. A group of four or six rectangular frames in a square shape works well.

Measuring correctly

If you're going to design a space, you need to know how to use a tape measure. Before dragging a piece of furniture to the other side of the room , it is best to know if it will fit. Either have someone hold the end of the tape measure for you or make sure you can hook onto something to get an accurate measurement. With the end secure, lay the tape measure on the floor as you pull it across the room. I always pull out as much as I think I may need and then add more to the tape as I need it to keep from making an inaccurate measurement.

Add color in the kitchen through staples and fruits.

Black-and-white poster size photos of favorite things such as your kids or pets fill up a large wall space. This can be done online at most major retailers offering photo services and picked up at the store or shipped to your home.

Do you have several small items you want to display? If you're a cottage or vintage style gal, try an old cola crate.

2: *Where are the Car Keys? Foyers*

YORK WALLCOVERINGS
800-375-YORK (9675); www.yorkwall.com

HUNTINGTON HOUSE
828-495-4400; www.huntingtonhouse.com

AMBELLA
14-748-5300; www.ambellahome.com

HOME ELEGANCE
www.homelegance.com

3: Take a Break! Living and Family Rooms

THAYER COGGIN
www.thayercoggin.com

FAIRFIELD CHAIR
828-758-5571; www.fairfieldchair.com

FURNITURELAND SOUTH
336-822-3000; www.furniturelandsouth.com

ENGLAND FURNITURE
423-626-5211; www.englandfurniture.com

COMFORTEX
800-843-4151; www.comfortex.com

HUNTINGTON HOUSE
828-495-4400; www.huntingtonhouse.com

HEKMAN CHAIR
616-748-2660; www.hekman.com

NAJARIAN FURNITURE
888-781-3088; www.najarianfurniture.com

YORK WALLCOVERINGS
800-375-9675; www.yorkwall.com

JENNIFER CONVERTIBLES
336-315-1980; www.jenniferfurniture.com

JONATHAN LOUIS
www.jonathanlouis.net

PALECEK
800-274-7730; www.palecek.com

LANEVENTURE
www.laneventure.com

BROOKS FURNITURE
800-427-6657; www.brooksfurnitureonline.com

BED BATH AND BEYOND
www.bedbathandbeyond.com

YORK WALLCOVERINGS
800-375-9675; www.yorkwall.com

FAIRFIELD CHAIR
828-758-5571; www.fairfieldchair.com

FURNITURE CLASSICS
888-325-7888; www.furnitureclassicsltd.com

LANEVENTURE
www.laneventure.com

MOEN
800-289-6636; www.moen.com

HOME ELEGANCE
www.homelegance.com

STAINLESS STEEL APPLIANCE FRONTS
www.applianceart.com

KITCHEN CRAFT CABINETRY
www.masterbrand.com

HEADBOARD DECALS
www.etsy.com

DURHAM FURNITURE INC.
519-369-2345; www.durhamfurnitures.com

FAIRFIELD CHAIR
828-758-5571; www.fairfieldchair.com

HOME TREASURES
713-937-7716; www.hometreasureslinens.com

YORK WALLCOVERINGS
800-375-9675; www.yorkwall.com

FURNITURELAND SOUTH
336-822-3000; www.furniturelandsouth.com

RAYMOND WAITES-NEXT CREATIONS HOLDINGS, LLC
212-447-8700; www.raymondwaites.com

ARIBISQUE

AMBELLA
214-748-5300; www.ambellahome.com

FURNITURE CLASSICS
888-325-7888; www.furnitureclassicsltd.com

7: Ahh, The Much Needed Bubble Bath: Bathrooms

AMBELLA
214-748-5300; www.ambellahome.com

CA INTERNATIONALS
www.bathsimple.com

MOEN
800-289-6636; www.moen.com

8: Go To Your Room: Children's Rooms

SOUTHEASTERN KIDS
336-884-1087; www.southeasternkids.com

FURNITURELAND SOUTH
336-822-3000; www.furniturelandsouth.com

CHROMCRAFT REVINGTON, INC.
www.chromcraft-revington.com

BOLTON FURNITURE
802-888-7974; www.boltonfurniture.biz

LEGACY KIDS
legacyclassickids.com

AMERICAN WOODCRAFTERS
336-861-0003; www.american-woodcrafters.com

YORK WALLCOVERINGS
800-375-9675; www.yorkwall.com

AMERICAN DREW
www.americandrew.com

BERG FURNITURE
www.bergfurniture.com

9: Beware of Falling Objects!
Playrooms and Workrooms

FURNITURELAND SOUTH
336-822-3000; www.furniturelandsouth.com

YORK WALLCOVERINGS
800-375-9675; www.yorkwall.com

WALL DECALS
www.etsy.com

10: Up, Up and Away! Displays

FURNITURELAND SOUTH
336-822-3000; www.furniturelandsouth.com

FURNITURE CLASSICS
888-325-7888; www.furnitureclassicsltd.com

HEKMAN CHAIR
616-748-2660; www.hekman.com

AMBELLA
214-748-5300; www.ambellahome.com

11: Tying it all Together

FURNITURE WALL STRAPS
www.amazon.com

KITCHEN CRAFT CABINETRY
www.masterbrand.com

DURHAM FURNITURE INC.
519-369-2345;
www.durhamfurnitures.com